SERIAL MOVIE POSTERS
volume ten of
the illustrated history of movies through posters

Images from the Hershenson-Allen Archive

Edited by Bruce Hershenson and Richard Allen
Published by Bruce Hershenson
P.O. Box 874, West Plains, MO 65775
Phone: 417 256 9616 Fax 417 257 6948
mail@brucehershenson.com (e-mail)
http://www.brucehershenson.com (website)

THE HERSHENSON-ALLEN ARCHIVE

Bruce Hershenson was the movie poster expert for Christie's auction house from 1990 to 1997, organizing ten auctions of rare vintage movie posters. In 1998 and 1999 he organized two auctions held at Howard Lowery Gallery. For all of these auctions he personally published a full-color catalog, similar to the volume you are holding in your hands. In all he has published twenty-one volumes of movie poster images. He has also issued sixteen semi-annual sales lists each containing thousands of posters. Bruce has professionally photographed the vast majority of posters and lobby cards he has had (over 15,000 items), so that they could be available for use in books, magazines and newspapers.

Richard Allen has long been one of the world's foremost collector's of vintage movie posters. He is the co-author (with Steve Rebello) of Reel Art, voted one of the hundred greatest books on film. He has gone to great lengths to track down rare and elusive images, and then has then restored and professionally photographed, so that they can be used in books, magazines and newspapers. His archive of images contains well over 15,000 images.

In 1997, Bruce Hershenson merged his archive with that of Richard Allen, created a joint archive that is unmatched anywhere in the world. The Hershenson-Allen Archive has over 25,000 different transparencies, covering a high percentage of all the film posters known to exist. Other sources offer some of the same images, but none offer them on high quality 4" by 5" color transparencies, every one of which is photographed directly from the original poster.

When you have a product that deserves the very finest possible reproduction, see what the Hershenson-Allen Archive can do for you. If you are a writer, publisher, or video producer, the archive is a wonderful resource which can greatly improve your product with eye catching images. The archive does not sell reproductions to individuals. These images are solely provided to publishers of books and magazines, and manufacturers of films, videos and discs. We have furnished hundreds of images for magazines such as Entertainment Weekly, newspapers such as The New York Times, books such as Time-Life Books, and even the U.S. Post Office. Whatever your need for full-color movie poster art, we can almost certainly help you.

You can reach the Hershenson-Allen Archive by phone at 417 256 9616, by fax at 417 257 6948, or online at http://www.brucehershenson.com.

INTRODUCTION

Welcome to the tenth volume of The Illustrated History of Movies Through Posters. This volume focuses on serials, the multi-chapter films that were shown in theaters (usually on a weekly basis). While it is very easy to identify the sound serials, it is not so easy when dealing with silent films. Most films of the teens were either one or two reels long, and there were often series of silent films, but these were not true serials.

A serial almost always had exactly ten, twelve, or fifteen chapters. It is a common misconception that every chapter of every serial ended with the hero or heroine in peril, closing with the words To Be Continued. Sometimes this happened, but sometimes not. When a chapter of a serial did end with a cliffhanger, they would sometimes 'cheat', and pick up the action in the next chapter in a slightly changed position.

Serials were first made in 1914, and one of the very first, and certainly the best-remembered, was The Perils of Pauline. They remained popular through the 1920s and the coming of sound only made serials even more popular. The two genres that adapted best to serials were cowboys and comic strip heroes, for serials needed non-stop action. Serials remained popular until the advent of television, for the serial concept was even better suited to TV, with a weekly show starring favorite action heroes.

It has been forty years since the last serial was filmed, yet there are still huge numbers of people who buy them on videos, and many of today's most popular films contain most of the elements that made serials so popular. The most successful film series ever, Star Wars, is a modern-day serial in which each chapter has been expanded into feature film length.

Unless otherwise noted, all of the images in this book are of the standard size movie poster, called a one-sheet and measuring 27" x 41". Other sizes include lobby cards (11" x 14"), three-sheets (41"x 81") and six-sheets (81" x 81"). Because serials had many chapters, many different one-sheets were made for each film. See the following page for more on this subject.

This series of books represents a quiet revolution in art book publishing. I believe most people would prefer to see more (and larger images) in art books, and will accept a paperback binding and forego the text material if it allows for better printing quality, and more images. Each of the books in this series contain as many images as most coffee table books, yet cost less than half as much and have better printing quality!

This is not a catalog of posters for sale, nor do I sell reproductions!! However I do sell posters of all kinds through sales catalogs and public auctions, so if you are interested in acquiring original vintage movie posters (or the other books I have published), visit my website at http://www.brucehershenson.com, or send me a self-addressed stamped envelope for free brochures.

I need to thank Richard Allen, my co-compiler in this book and many previous volumes. He continually tracks down elusive images that greatly enrich this series. I also need to thank Sylvia Hershenson, who proofread this book and prepared the index and cutlines; Amy Regez of Sullivan/Santamaria Design, who did the layout and designed the cover; and the printer, Courier Graphics.

I dedicate this book to my newly-arrived third child, Hayley Suzanne Hershenson. I did not become a father until I was nearly forty, and my children have added immeasurably to my life!

Bruce Hershenson
August 1999

ATTENTION ALL SERIAL POSTER COLLECTORS!!

I am sure that many of the people who will buy this book own one or more original serial movie posters. I am asking you to help in what I believe is a most worthwhile project. Please read the following if you own any serial posters, or know of someone who does.

Most of the books I have published deal with a genre that contains many thousands of films. I could never hope to publish every horror image or every cowboy image, for there are far too many of those films. But there are only a limited number of serials (approximately five hundred, half sound and half silent). I am going to publish a sequel to this volume that contains images from those serials that are not represented here. It may not be possible to find images from every one of the silent serials, but I should certainly be able to obtain all of the sound ones.

In addition, I would like to show different posters from the serials that are included in this volume. For most serials, there was a different one-sheet for every chapter. Sometimes there would be an extra "stock" poster for the entire serial, which would often be full artwork and have a great full-color image. (If there wasn't a stock poster, then often the Chapter One one-sheet was a full-color full artwork poster.) Sometimes several of the other chapters would have differing images, but most often the posters for many (sometimes all) of the chapters would have the same basic image with an insert area that would show a duotone scene from each particular chapter.

You'll find examples of all of these different types of posters in this volume. If I only picture a chapter poster, then I am looking for the stock poster, and any different style chapter posters, and if I picture only the stock poster, then I am looking for however many different chapter styles there were.

So if you have (or know of) any posters that are different from those shown in this book, please contact me at once. If you'll allow me to borrow them and have them professionally photographed for the sequel (at my expense), I'll give you a free copy of the book and prominently credit you in it. I would also like to borrow full-color lobby cards from serials (some serials had them, but many didn't), as well as images of any other size posters. The only posters that don't appear in this book that I don't want to borrow are one-sheets that are only different in that they have different insets from those that are pictured here.

If everyone in the hobby will join in, I will be able to publish a spectacular second volume, which together with the first volume will form a comprehensive encyclopedia of serial films. If you have posters you are willing to lend (or if you want to be notified when the second volume is ready), contact me at the address or phone number on the title page of this volume.

Bruce Hershenson
August 1999

1. THE PERILS OF PAULINE, 1914

2. THE PERILS OF PAULINE, 1914

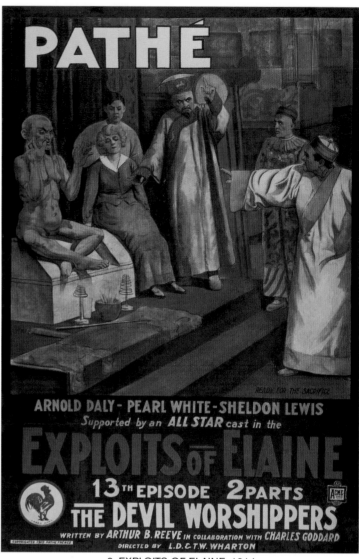

3. EXPLOITS OF ELAINE, 1914

4. THE AMATEUR DETECTIVE, 1914

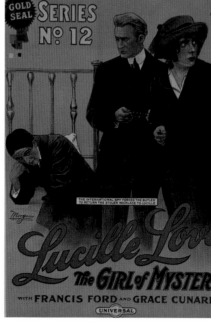

5. LUCILLE LOVE, 1914

6. A RAILROADER'S BRAVERY, 1914

7. THE SHIELDING SHADOW, 1916

8. THE RAILROAD RAIDERS, 1917

9. SMASHING BARRIERS, 1919

10. THE GREAT GAMBLE, 1919

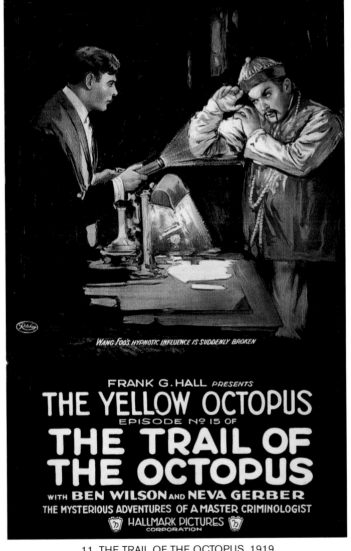

11. THE TRAIL OF THE OCTOPUS, 1919

12. THE MASTER MYSTERY, 1919

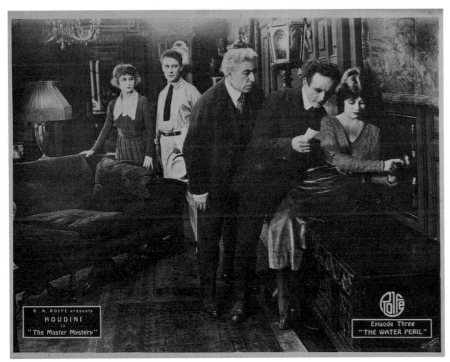

13. THE MASTER MYSTERY, 1919, lobby card

14. THE LION MAN, 1919

15. A SOCIETY HOLD-UP, 1919, three-sheet

16. ELMO THE MIGHTY, 1919, Title card

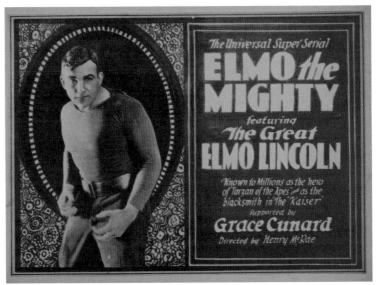

17. ELMO THE MIGHTY, 1919, Title card

18. THE SON OF TARZAN, 1920

19. THE SON OF TARZAN, 1920

20. ELMO THE FEARLESS, 1920

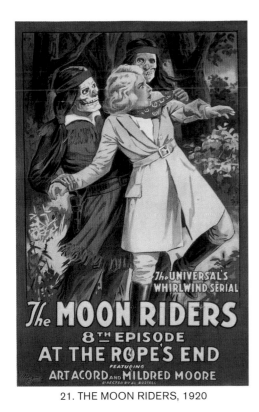

21. THE MOON RIDERS, 1920

22. VELVET FINGERS, 1920

23. THE LOST CITY, 1920

24. MIRACLES OF THE JUNGLE, 1921

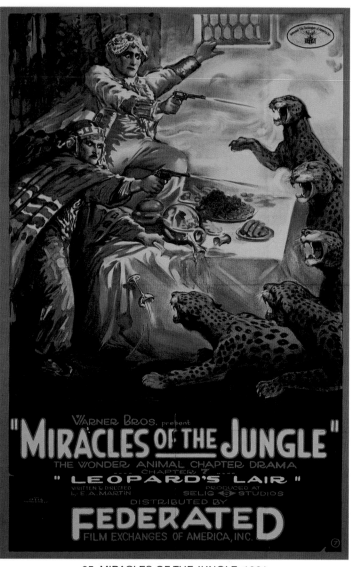

25. MIRACLES OF THE JUNGLE, 1921

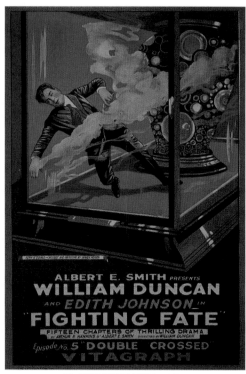

26. FIGHTING FATE, 1921

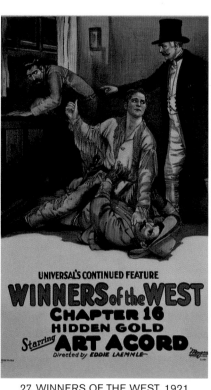

27. WINNERS OF THE WEST, 1921

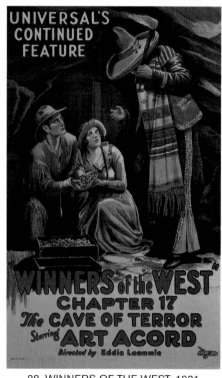

28. WINNERS OF THE WEST, 1921

29. ADVENTURES OF TARZAN, 1921, window card

30. WHITE EAGLE, 1922

31. SPEED, 1922

32. IN THE DAYS OF BUFFALO BILL, 1922

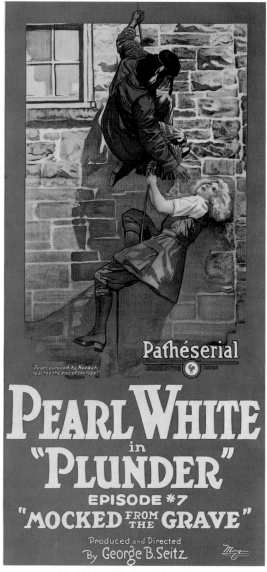

33. PLUNDER, 1922, three-sheet

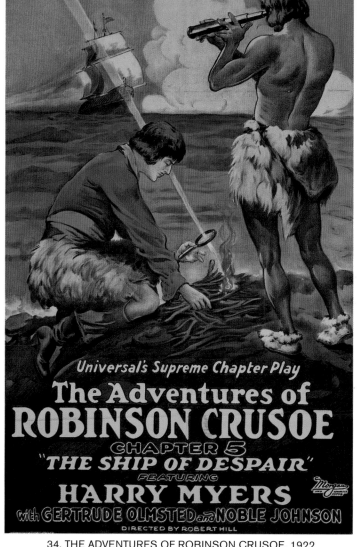

34. THE ADVENTURES OF ROBINSON CRUSOE, 1922

35. THE ADVENTURES OF ROBINSON CRUSOE, 1922

36. HAUNTED VALLEY, 1923, special poster

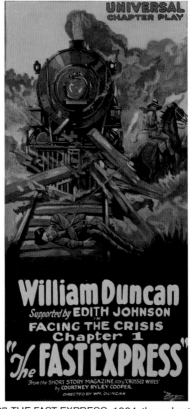

37. THE FAST EXPRESS, 1924, three-sheet

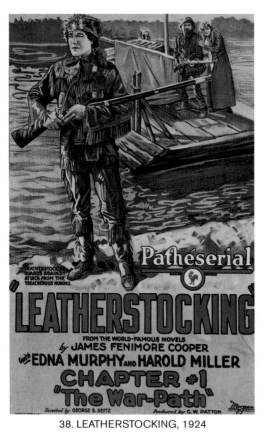

38. LEATHERSTOCKING, 1924

39. PERILS OF THE WILD, 1925

40. THE FIGHTING MARINE, 1926

41. TARZAN THE MIGHTY, 1928

42. THE RADIO DETECTIVE, 1926

43. THE WINKING IDOL, 1926

44. THE FATAL WARNING, 1929

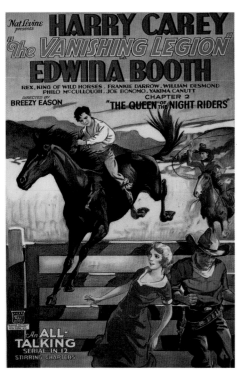

45. THE VANISHING LEGION, 1931

46. THE PHANTOM OF THE WEST, 1931

47. THE GALLOPING GHOST, 1931

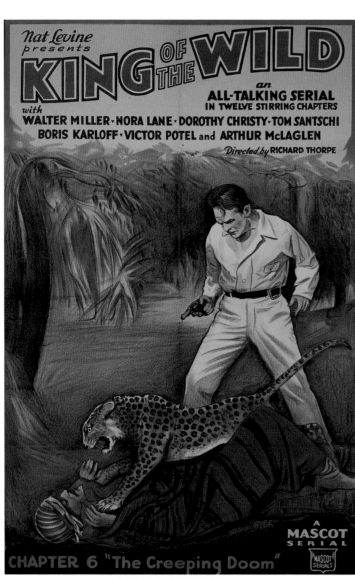

48. KING OF THE WILD, 1931

49. THE HURRICANE EXPRESS, 1932

50. GORDON OF GHOST CITY, 1933

51. THE THREE MUSKETEERS, 1933

52. FIGHTING WITH KIT CARSON, 1933

53. THE MYSTERY SQUADRON, 1933, Title card

54. THE WOLF DOG, 1933

55. TARZAN THE FEARLESS, 1933, three-sheet

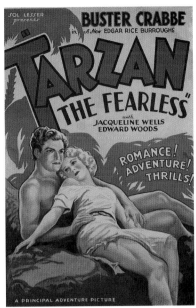

56. TARZAN THE FEARLESS, 1933

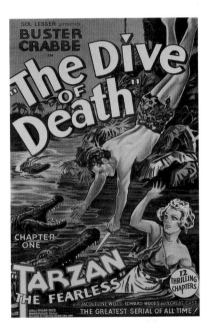

57. TARZAN THE FEARLESS, 1933

58. TARZAN THE FEARLESS, 1933

59. THE LOST JUNGLE, 1934, Title card

62. BURN 'EM UP BARNES, 1934

60. THE LOST JUNGLE, 1934, lobby card

61. THE LOST JUNGLE, 1934, lobby card

63. BURN 'EM UP BARNES, 1934

64. MYSTERY MOUNTAIN, 1934, six-sheet

65. MYSTERY MOUNTAIN, 1934

66. MYSTERY MOUNTAIN, 1934

67. MYSTERY MOUNTAIN, 1934, Title card

68. THE RETURN OF CHANDU, 1934

69. THE RETURN OF CHANDU, 1934

70. CHANDU ON THE MAGIC ISLAND, 1934

71. THE RETURN OF CHANDU, 1934, three-sheet

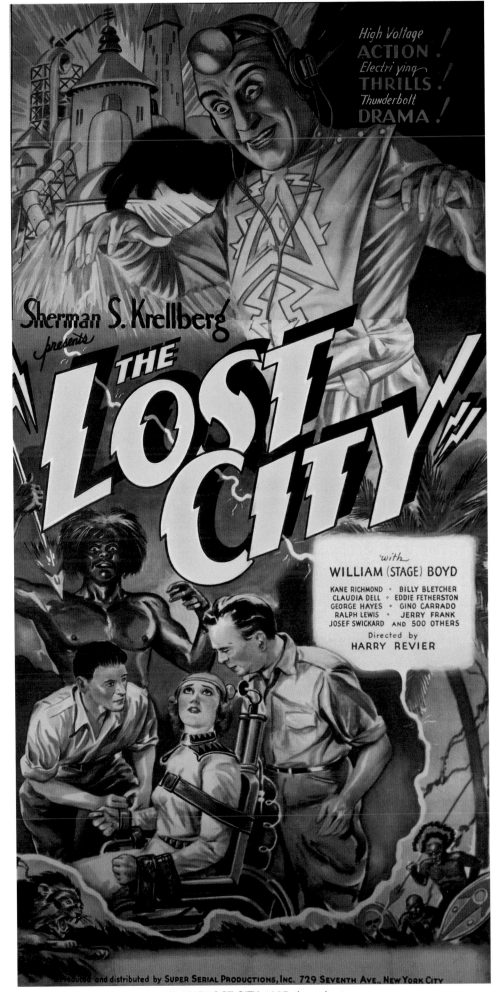

72. THE LOST CITY, 1935, three-sheet

73. THE LOST CITY, 1935

74. THE LOST CITY, 1935

75. THE ADVENTURES OF REX
AND RINTY, 1935

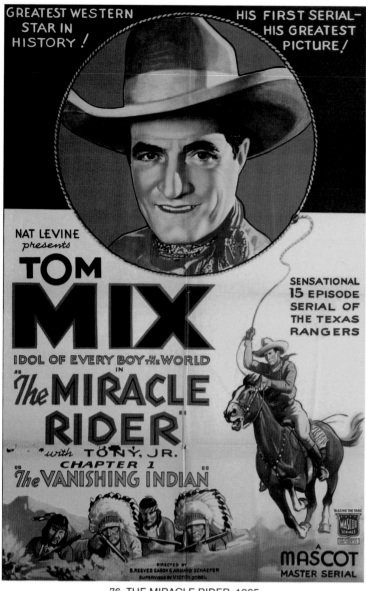

76. THE MIRACLE RIDER, 1935

77. THE MIRACLE RIDER, 1935, Title card

78. THE MIRACLE RIDER, 1935, lobby card

79. THE MIRACLE RIDER, 1935

80. THE MIRACLE RIDER, 1935

81. THE MIRACLE RIDER, 1935

82. THE MIRACLE RIDER, 1935

83. THE MIRACLE RIDER, 1935

84. THE MIRACLE RIDER, 1935

85. THE MIRACLE RIDER, 1935, three-sheet

86. THE PHANTOM EMPIRE, 1935

87. THE PHANTOM EMPIRE, 1935

88. THE PHANTOM EMPIRE, 1935

89. THE PHANTOM EMPIRE, 1935, three-sheet

90. THE PHANTOM EMPIRE, 1935, set of eight lobby cards

91. FIGHTING MARINES, 1935

92. THE NEW ADVENTURES OF TARZAN, 1935

93. UNDERSEA KINGDOM, 1936

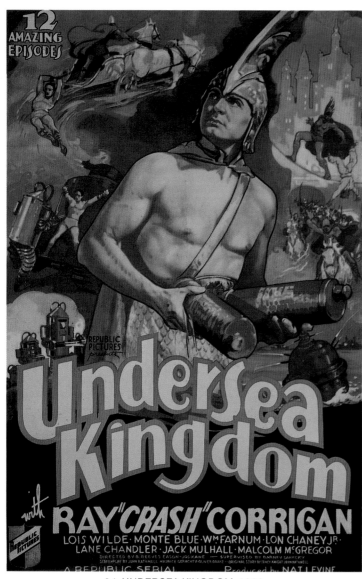

94. UNDERSEA KINGDOM, 1936

95. UNDERSEA KINGDOM, 1936

96. FLASH GORDON, 1936

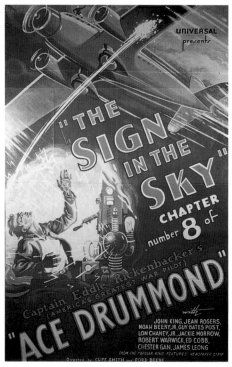

97. ACE DRUMMOND, 1936

98. THE PHANTOM RIDER, 1936

99. THE VIGILANTES ARE COMING, 1936

100. DARKEST AFRICA, 1936

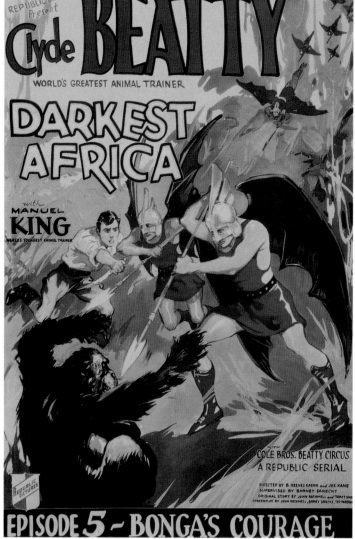

101. DARKEST AFRICA, 1936

102. DARKEST AFRICA, 1936

103. ROBINSON CRUSOE OF
CLIPPER ISLAND, 1936

104. SHADOW OF CHINATOWN, 1936

105. SHADOW OF CHINATOWN, 1936

106. SHADOW OF CHINATOWN, 1936, three-sheet

107. JUNGLE JIM, 1936

108. ZORRO RIDES AGAIN, 1937

109. SOS COAST GUARD, 1937

110. THE MYSTERIOUS PILOT, 1937

111. BLAKE OF SCOTLAND YARD, 1937

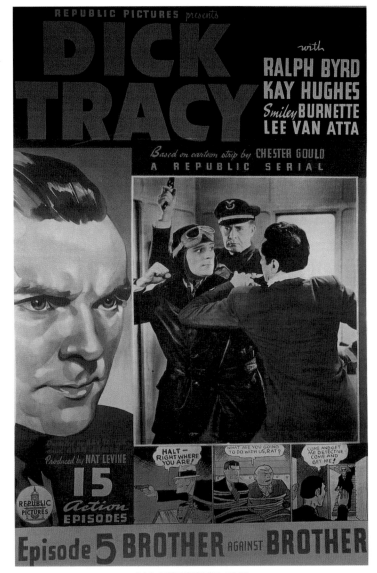

112. DICK TRACY, 1937

113. DICK TRACY, 1937

114. SECRET AGENT X-9, 1937

115. TIM TYLER'S LUCK, 1937

116. RED BARRY, 1938

117. THE FIGHTING DEVIL DOGS, 1938

118. HAWK OF THE WILDERNESS, 1938

119. THE LONE RANGER, 1938

120. THE LONE RANGER, 1938

121. DICK TRACY RETURNS, 1938

122. FLASH GORDON'S TRIP TO MARS, 1938

123. FLASH GORDON'S TRIP TO MARS, 1938

124. FLASH GORDON'S TRIP TO MARS, 1938

125. FLASH GORDON'S TRIP TO MARS, 1938

126. FLAMING FRONTIERS, 1938

127. FLAMING FRONTIERS, 1938

128. DICK TRACY'S G-MEN, 1939

129. MANDRAKE THE MAGICIAN, 1939

130. THE PHANTOM CREEPS, 1939

131. THE PHANTOM CREEPS, 1939

132. DAREDEVILS OF THE RED CIRCLE, 1939

133. THE GREEN HORNET, 1939

134. THE LONE RANGER RIDES AGAIN, 1939

135. THE GREEN HORNET STRIKES AGAIN, 1940

136. THE LONE RANGER RIDES AGAIN, 1939

137. ZORRO'S FIGHTING LEGION, 1939

138. DEADWOOD DICK, 1940

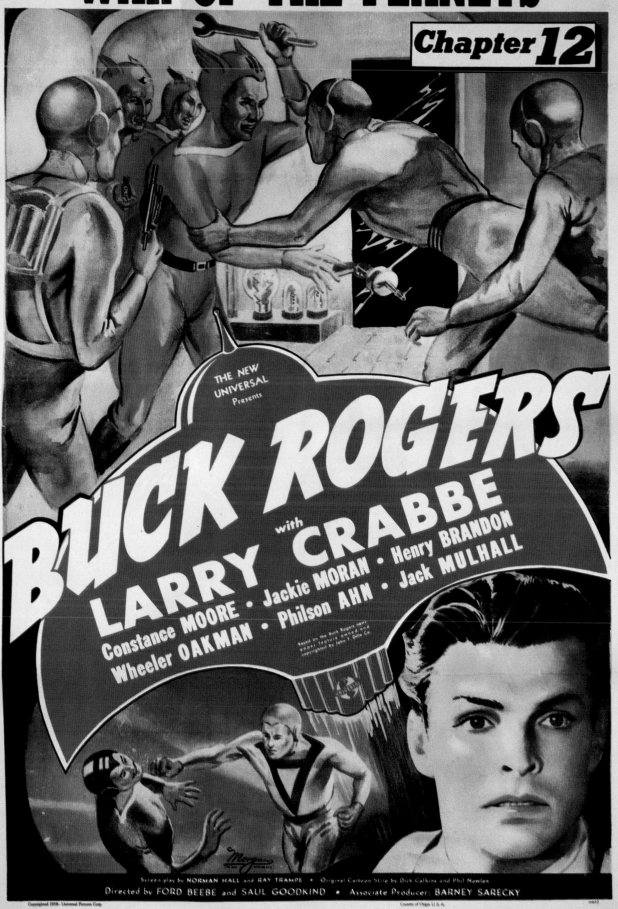

139. BUCK ROGERS, 1940

140. FLASH GORDON CONQUERS THE UNIVERSE, 1940

141. FLASH GORDON CONQUERS THE UNIVERSE, 1940

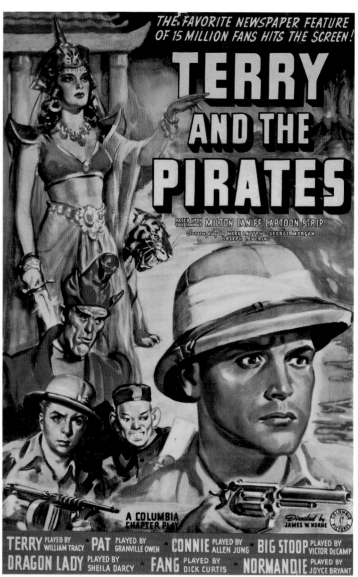

142. TERRY AND THE PIRATES, 1940

143. DRUMS OF FU MANCHU, 1940

144. JUNIOR G-MEN, 1940

145. DICK TRACY VS. CRIME INC., 1941

146. ADVENTURES OF CAPTAIN MARVEL, 1941, six-sheet

147. ADVENTURES OF CAPTAIN MARVEL, 1941

148. ADVENTURES OF CAPTAIN MARVEL, 1941

149. THE IRON CLAW, 1941

150. JUNGLE GIRL, 1941

151. THE SPIDER RETURNS, 1941

152. HOLT OF THE SECRET SERVICE, 1942

153. THE VALLEY OF VANISHING MEN, 1942

154. PERILS OF THE ROYAL MOUNTED, 1942

155. CAPTAIN MIDNIGHT, 1942, three-sheet

156. SPY SMASHER, 1942

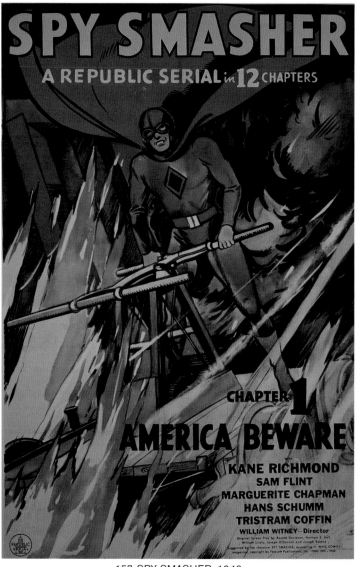

157. SPY SMASHER, 1942

158. SPY SMASHER, 1942

159. PERILS OF NYOKA, 1942

160. PERILS OF NYOKA, 1942

161. JUNIOR G-MEN OF THE AIR, 1942

162. OVERLAND MAIL, 1942

163. ADVENTURES OF THE FLYING CADETS, 1943

164. DAREDEVILS OF THE WEST, 1943

165. THE ADVENTURES OF SMILIN' JACK, 1943

166. THE PHANTOM, 1943

167. THE SHADOW, 1943 (This poster is from the 1947 reissue of this film. If anyone has anything from this film dated 1943 contact me immediately!)

168. THE BATMAN, 1943

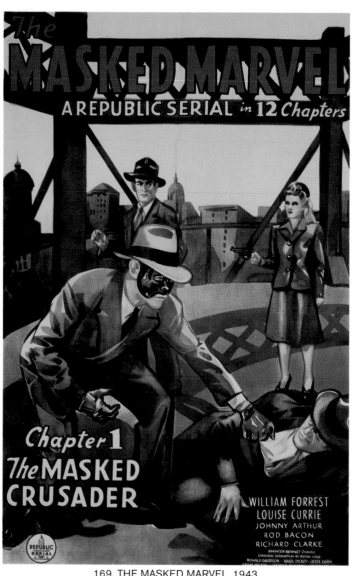

169. THE MASKED MARVEL, 1943

170. G-MEN VS. THE BLACK DRAGON, 1943

171. THE MASKED MARVEL, 1943

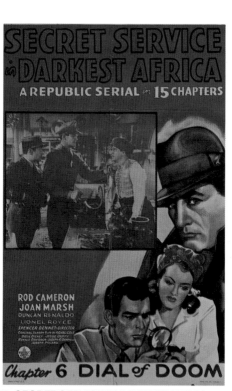

172. SECRET SERVICE IN DARKEST AFRICA, 1943

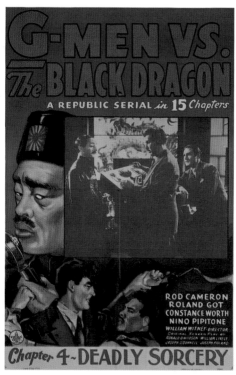

173. G-MEN VS. THE BLACK DRAGON, 1943

174. THE TIGER WOMAN, 1944

175. BLACK ARROW, 1944, six-sheet

176. HAUNTED HARBOR, 1944

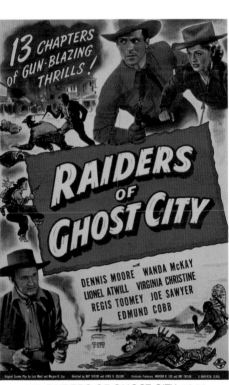

177. RAIDERS OF GHOST CITY, 1944

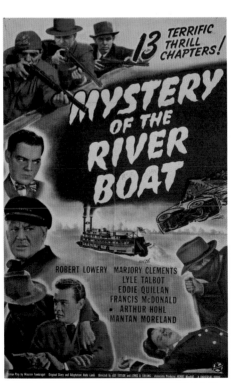

178. MYSTERY OF THE RIVER BOAT, 1944

179. CAPTAIN AMERICA, 1944

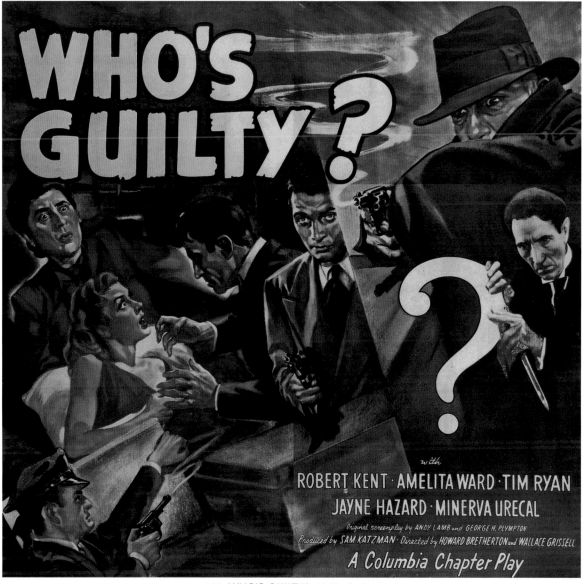

180. WHO'S GUILTY?, 1945, six-sheet

181. JUNGLE QUEEN, 1945

182. ZORRO'S BLACK WHIP, 1945

183. THE MONSTER AND THE APE, 1945

184. KING OF THE FOREST RANGERS, 1946

185. THE PHANTOM RIDER, 1946

186. ADVENTURES OF FRANK AND JESSE JAMES, 1948

187. CONGO BILL, 1948

188. G-MEN NEVER FORGET, 1948

189. SUPERMAN, 1948

190. SUPERMAN, 1948, six-sheet

191. SUPERMAN, 1948, three-sheet

192. SUPERMAN, 1948

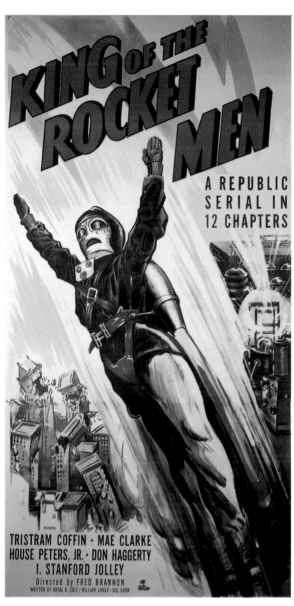

193. KING OF THE ROCKET MEN, 1949

194. KING OF THE ROCKET MEN, 1949, three-sheet

195. THE ADVENTURES OF SIR GALAHAD, 1949

196. GHOST OF ZORRO, 1949

197. BRUCE GENTRY, 1949

198. NEW ADVENTURES OF BATMAN AND ROBIN, 1949

199. NEW ADVENTURES OF BATMAN AND ROBIN, 1949, six-sheet

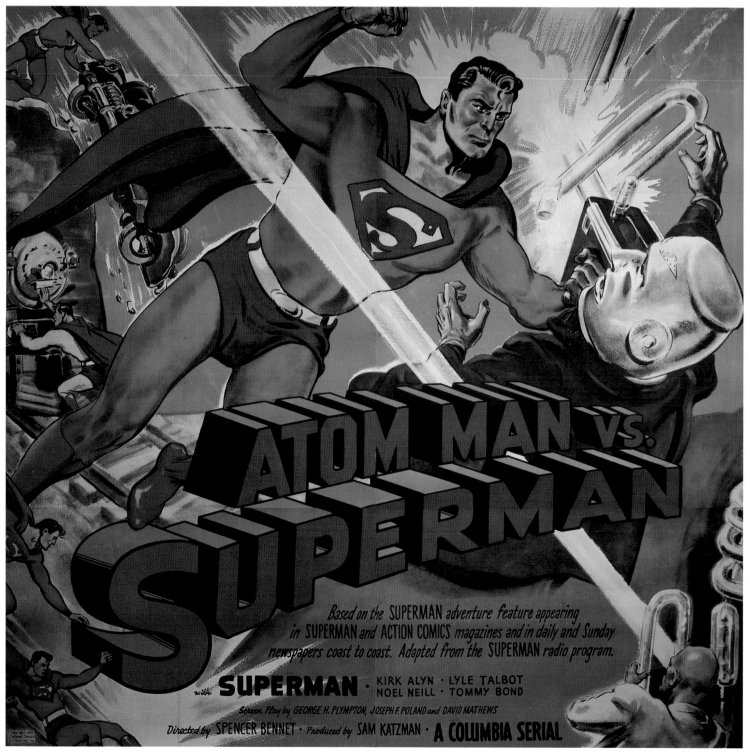

200. ATOM MAN VS. SUPERMAN, 1950, six-sheet

201. ATOM MAN VS. SUPERMAN, 1950, three-sheet

202. ATOM MAN VS. SUPERMAN, 1950

203. RADAR PATROL VS. SPY KING, 1950

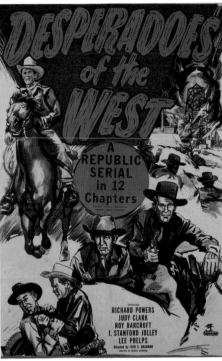

204. DESPERADOES OF THE WEST, 1950

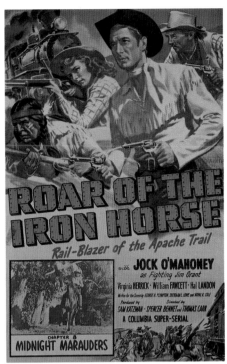

205. ROAR OF THE IRON HORSE, 1951

206. ROAR OF THE IRON HORSE, 1951, three-sheet

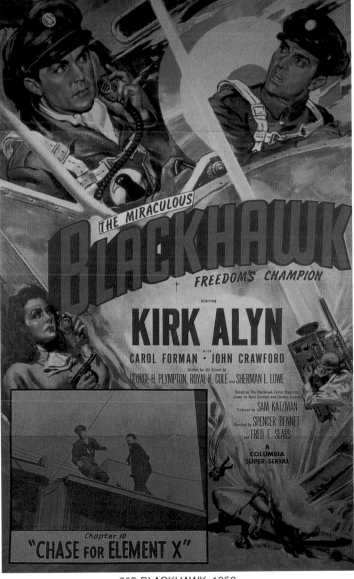

207. BLACKHAWK, 1952

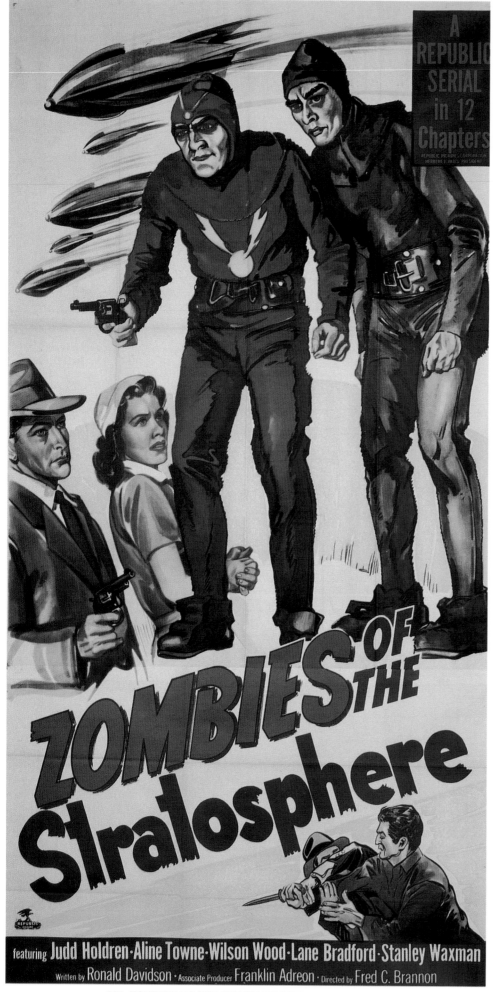

208. ZOMBIES OF THE STRATOSPHERE, 1952, three-sheet

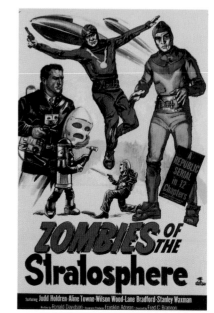

209. ZOMBIES OF THE STRATOSPHERE, 1952

210. KING OF THE CONGO, 1952

211. COMMANDO CODY, 1953

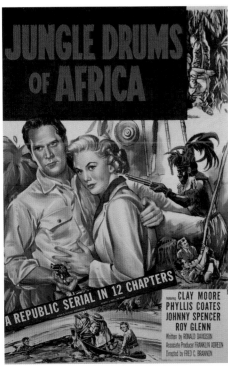

212. JUNGLE DRUMS OF AFRICA, 1953

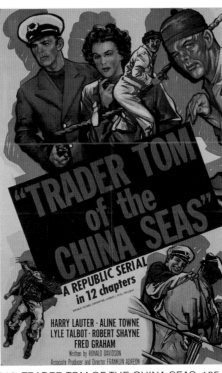

213. TRADER TOM OF THE CHINA SEAS, 1954

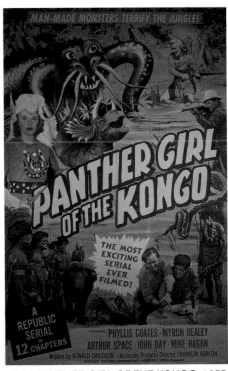

214. PANTHER GIRL OF THE KONGO, 1955

215. ADVENTURES OF CAPTAIN AFRICA

216. BLAZING THE OVERLAND TRAIL, 1956

SERIAL MOVIE POSTERS

SERIAL MOVIE POSTERS

STILL AVAILABLE! ORDER DIRECT FROM THE PUBLISHER OR CHECK YOUR LOCAL BOOKSTORE. . . IF THEY DON'T HAVE THEM IN STOCK, THEY CAN BE SPECIAL ORDERED.

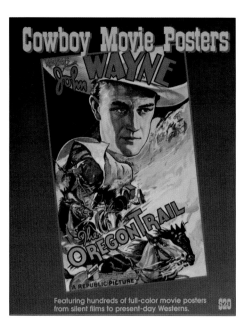

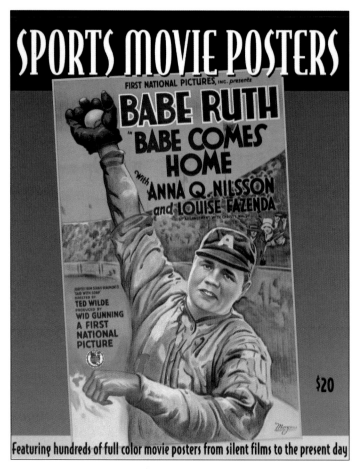

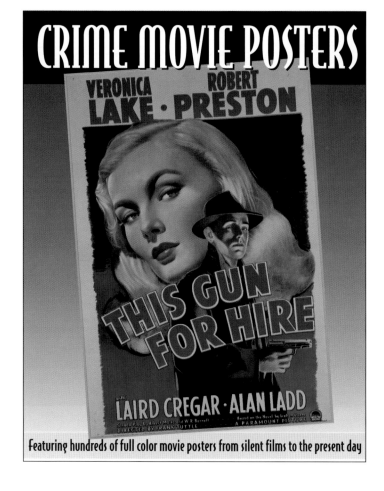

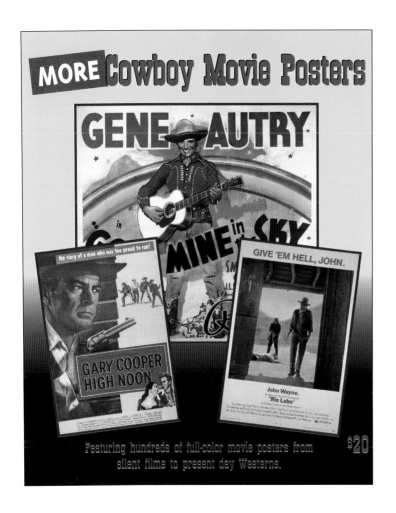

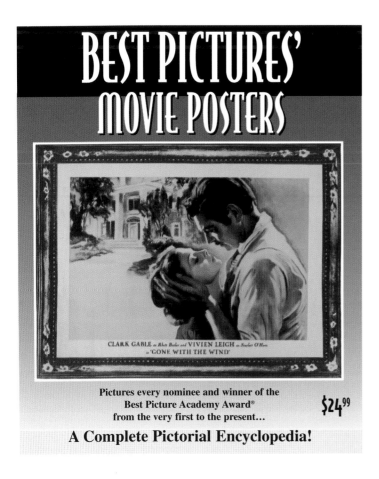

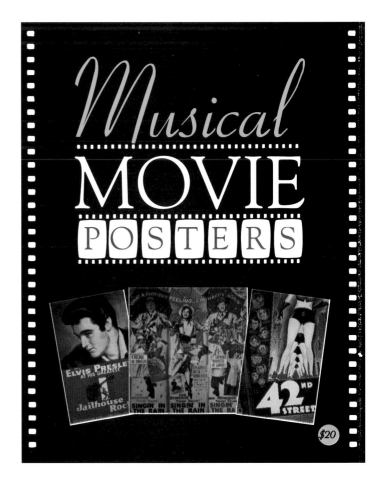